TRUST IT WORKS

The future is there for those who believe in their affirmations

TOM McCRORY

outskirtspress

DENVER, COLORADO

Outskirts Press, Inc.
http://www.outskirtspress.com

ISBN: 978-1-4787-0865-0

Outskirts Press and the "OP" logo are trademarks belonging to Outskirts Press, Inc.

PRINTED IN THE UNITED STATES OF AMERICA

TABLE OF CONTENTS

ACKNOWLEDGEMENTS

This book would not have been written in the time that it has if it was not for my wonderful wife Pat and her excellent typing skills. She has typed and checked at least four draft copies of this book and I thank her most sincerely for her time, patience and effort.

I would also like to thank a very dear friend of mine – Kay E Phipps, BeD who took the time to appraise the contents of this book in a critical and constructive way.

A PERSONAL MESSAGE FROM TOM

No matter what and who you are you have the right to be who you would like to be, and to have all the things in life that will bring you happiness, health, wealth, peace, balance and harmony. I was brought up in an inner city slum area of Leeds. Five families shared the same house and my mother had to wait her turn to do the cooking on one of the two gas stoves in the house. My playground was the derelict houses nearby. During my childhood I found myself living in care homes. I left school when I was fifteen and I was a shy, nervous young man with no confidence and few skills.

I became an engineer and even though I struggled and had to take some exams twice, I finally made the grade. It was during this period that I came across an article in a magazine. The topic was *Destiny and Fate*. Little did I realise that many years later I would realise that we are all co-creators in life and we each have the ability to attract into our lives what it is we desire.

Trust me; you can create a better life for yourself. I have written this book from my own experiences and knowledge that has come to me from many sources including books, magazines and talks. One thing in common with all my sources was the fact that what I was listening to and reading confirmed what I was already aware of and practising, the greatest of which was my knowing that I could create and attract into my life, those positive energies that bring happiness, health, peace and those inner goals and desires that we all have.

Today's thoughts are tomorrow's actions and attractions. Make your thoughts positive and attract into your life, your goals and desires. Don't forget to look at the back of the book where you will find your own goals and desires chart. This will give you a record of when and what goal and or desire came to fruition.

The Wisdom of a Father.

One day a father caught his son pulling up his plants in the garden. He said "son you pull out a plant and you pull out its potential to grow". Your own goals and desires are like the plants. Don't pull them out before they have grown.

INTRODUCTION

Change your mind and change your life

This book on affirmations you are now holding in your hand could change your life forever.
Everyone has some kind of goal or desire they
would like to achieve in their life. Goals and
desires can be anything from finding peace and
happiness to finding the right job, career or relationship or it could be financial prosperity and
success in your chosen field. Whatever your goal
or desire is, this book will guide you in the right
direction, explaining what affirmations are and
how their powerful message can attract into your
life your personal goals and desires. Once you
have experienced the success of attracting goals
and desires into your life you will never be the
same person again. You will have applied the

techniques of affirming, found them to work and become one of the families whose first affirmation is *Trust me it works*.

To maximise your potential for success the opening chapters are entitled **Within You is the Power** (Chapter 1) and **The Spiritual Laws of Life** (Chapter 3). These chapters give you an explanation as to why you are the person you are today and that you do have a wonderful hidden power within, something that once accessed, can change your life forever. You can become who you would like to be and not what others want you to be. Spiritual laws are those timeless virtues and values of life that have always been around – virtues such as kindness, compassion, gratitude and patience.

Used positively, these laws can support and add power to your goals and desires by *VIRTUE* of the fact that what goes around comes around. For example, if you always show kindness to others, others will show kindness to you. When you are patient with others, others become patient with you. Your kindness and patience has attracted into your life, that which you have given out. It really pays to embrace the Spiritual laws of life.

CHAPTER 1
WITHIN YOU IS
THE POWER

Throughout history mention has been made of the energy of the power within. It has been called the *power of life, the power within, the power of the universe.* Today it is generally known and called *the power of the mind.* Even though we know far more about the mind we still find it hard to maximise its potential.

We talk about using only a portion of the *power of the mind* and yet we each have the potential to access to a greater degree, this power within which I believe is part of a greater power which I call *the Great Spirit or the energy of life* and some call *god or creator.* It is important to recognise that we are all part of the energy of life. It is with and within us. It is in all that you see, feel, smell, sense and hear. It is nature and all the creatures of the land, air and sea. It is the power that creates the galaxies and the stars. It is the energy of all life.

I believe this power, this energy, is the voice of the universe and it has one message – *trust me I work only for your highest good. How may I serve you?* There are many reasons why so many people in our world find it hard to attract, achieve and create what they would like in their life. This first chapter helps you to recognise why this is so and gives you the opportunity to turn your life around - to perceive things in a different way, to be who you desire to be. SO!! Where do we start this amazing journey of unfolding your hidden potential?

To seek the answer as to why we feel, act, think and do the things we do, we have to go back to our early childhood and formative years. Historically it is during this period that generally our beliefs and conditioning of our mind is established by the various social structures built into our family and society. I call this. . . . .

(**The Social Circle of Life**) and within this circle are the reasons why we feel trapped and unable to break free. Understanding how we can change our minds and change our life helps us break this social circle of entrapment.

The Social Circle of Life

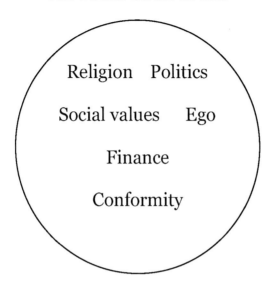

Religion   Politics

Social values   Ego

Finance

Conformity

Generally we are taught within our own family and social system that this is the way things are and we are expected to believe and follow the rules of the family and social system.

The majority of people have been moulded and fashioned by their families and the social system to such a degree that they act and think according to the values of them, especially where the media is concerned, where people read, listen and generally accept what is said to be the truth! Being creatures of habit, people do not think that there may be more to what they are led to believe, or that there may be a better way for them to do things. If you do think of a better way it is often frowned upon by the family and social system. It is looked upon as being non-conformist, radical, extreme, or just plain anti-social.

One example of this would be your religious and political values based on your family's beliefs. You begin to realise, as many do, that you were not given a choice – you were told that, "this is your religion" or "this is the political party you must vote for". The same goes for many social and environmental issues, for example, conformity within our society. Dress, act and work as everyone else does and it is fine, but change your views radically, change your hairstyle/music or dress radically and society looks upon you as someone different, i.e. you are stereotyped and catalogued when all the time all that you desire is to be yourself. Many people have a great fear of becoming who or what they want to be, for one simple thought –*but what will my family and friends think?* They worry about what their families will think of them if they want to change their religious beliefs, or political views, or even if they want to dye their hair blue or green. They worry if they come from a poor background and have good ideas to create wealth but their families or friends tell them they will never make it.

People who see themselves as thin, ugly or over-weight, listen too much to those who say, "You will never find a suitable partner." Someone with a poor education may listen to others too much when they are told that they will, "Never make the grade." The list is endless for lost opportunities holding us back either because our family and/or society may say to us, *"No, you're not doing that"* or you think, **but what will they think?**

Does some or all of this relate to you now or did it in the past? Remember we are like we are as a result of how we have been moulded by past events, but as from now you can choose to change your mind and change your life.

Affirmations

Affirmations have been around for a long time and have been used successfully by many people who recognised through positive experiences, that when they continually focused their mind positively on something they desired, it turned up in their life. They may not have understood how it worked but it did and they built a belief system around this.

With today's knowledge and understanding of the mind, we know that affirmations work and by wording your affirmation in such a way, it acts like a call sign to the universe which responds – *How May I Serve You?* (Trust me it works!)

To maximise your potential for success through affirmations, it is of positive benefit to look at and observe certain guidelines. The definition of an affirmation is '*A statement made by you mentally and repeated on a regular basis, verbally, mentally or in written form.*' To gain an understanding of how they work and why repeating them helps to create what you are looking for, it is useful to look at the basic concepts of the power of our mind as this is where the process of self-creating begins.

A STATEMENT WITH ENERGY

"Something positive is about

to happen in my life

and I feel good

about it"

CHAPTER 2
WHERE DO WE START?

Not everyone desires to be a doctor or engineer, but we all have that inner desire to change and improve our lives and realise our goals and desires.

Our thoughts are living energies. As we think then so we are. Therefore we can control and direct our thoughts to the power within. Direct them wisely and today's thoughts will become tomorrow's actions.

The secret to accessing the energy of the power within is to recognise that your thoughts are living energies and as you think so you are and so it is. **YOU** can control and direct your own thoughts. Try this quick example. Think of your house number or name! By the time you have read this instruction I bet you had already brought to your mind the name or number! **YOU** controlled and directed your thoughts to obtain this information. When you learn to direct your thoughts wisely, today's thoughts will become your tomorrow's actions and attractions for what it is you wish to manifest.

How does it work?

It works by being connected to the energy of life which has all the power we need to grow and develop physically, materially, and spiritually in all areas.

Are you connected to this energy of life?

On the following page you will find what I call comfort and discomfort zones. These zones indicate what areas of your life cause you to feel connected **or** disconnected to that force or power of life. Compare each zone. Where do you feel **you** fit in at this moment of time? Of course there are many more examples than these but at least you can begin to understand why you feel the way you do sometimes. The following pages give clear direction as to how you can move more into your comfort zone and reconnect with the power of the mind.

IDEAL COMFORT ZONE

(Balanced)

Peace - Comfort - Gratitude

Spiritual and Religious beliefs

Food – Warmth - Shelter

Good Job - Good Health

Good Family – Friends

Financial Security

Direction in life

Confidence

Self Worth

DISCOMFORT ZONE

(Unbalanced)

Insecurity - Fear - Uncertainty

Lack of belief and self respect

Past life experiences - Stress

Cannot forgive or forget

Feeling all alone in life

Can't let go of the past

Anger - Poor health

Lack of direction

No job

THE POWER OF YOUR MIND

HOW IT WORKS

<u>A</u>

You are in charge. You direct and control your thoughts.

<u>B</u>

Your subconscious obeys the commands from the power of your thoughts.

<u>C</u>

The result: you experience the outcome and you create your desire, goal or habit.

To know how to access **the power within**, you need to understand the basic concepts of your conscious and subconscious mind. Your conscious mind **A** is that which deals with thinking, analysing, judging, decision-making, imagination, awareness and perception. Think of this part of the mind as your planning and design office – the place where **your** ideas and thoughts originate.

Your subconscious mind **B** is that part of the mind which lacks the faculties of reasoning, judging, thinking, analysing and perceiving. The subconscious mind has only the power to obey or respond to repeated commands or instinctive stimuli.

For example, if you put your hand on a hot surface the subconscious mind instinctively responds automatically, i.e. you move your hand away without even thinking. Conditionally, your subconscious mind takes in all forms of information from the world. Some examples would be Television, Radio, Ipods, place of work, the crowded shopping mall. We live in a noisy and fast-living world where we do not seem to have a quiet moment to ourselves. All this information or stimuli enters our subconscious and remains there as what I call, brain junk, until such a time comes when repeated commands or stimuli create a response. For instance being bombarded with an advert for a chocolate bar - you end up buying it, liking it and buying it again and again which represents that motivating force known as habit, i.e. we have a result **C** and created a desire, goal or habit and of course the advertisers have done a good job!

Habits

Habits are those things in life that remind us it is time again to have another drink, have a smoke, bite your nails, look at the clock, eat some chocolate etc. We are creatures of habit and to a greater or lesser degree some people have habits which they appear to have no control over as a result of repeated commands to the subconscious. Generally the main ones we think about are smoking and drinking. Understanding the relationship between habits and your subconscious is the secret to enjoying this book and changing your life. Habits form when we repeatedly say or do something so often that we programme our subconscious mind with a repeat message which it can only obey by reminding our conscious mind that it is time once more to smoke, drink, eat etc. We respond to our conscious mind with the craving or feeling – *I need a cigarette/drink/a piece of chocolate etc*.

Knowing that our habits are formed in this way gives us a clue as to how we can improve and change our life for the better. As you read earlier, your conscious mind is that which thinks, imagines and plans ideas.

Your subconscious mind can only obey repeated commands, and can with your instructions, create in your life the positive ideas that you condition it with. I believe that our subconscious mind has a direct link with the energy of life itself which recognises the repeated commands that it receives and acts upon them just like the habits mentioned. Habits are hard to break as we all know.

This same rule applies to good habits also. By creating good, positive habits you will find that when you need help the most, your helpful habits will appear and give you the strength and support you need. Positive affirmations are good habits and have a wonderful way of making things happen. They can help to reduce stress, induce peace and calm and help attract into your life that which you desire.

THE POWER OF YOUR MIND

IS THE DOORWAY TO

RECONNECTING

YOU TO THE ENERGY OF LIFE

CHANGE YOUR MIND AND CHANGE

YOUR LIFE.

THIS IS THE KEY THAT YOU NEED

TO OPEN

THE DOORS OF YOUR MIND

Affirmation and Feelings

It is said that our **feelings** are the truest representation of how we are at any moment in our life and I believe this wholeheartedly. How do you *feel* at this moment? Happy - Sad – Well - Upset - Positive - Nervous - Anxious – Excited?

How you *feel* inside is a sure sign of how you *feel* life is treating you on the outside. Trust me you do have the power to change your life by changing your mind which changes your *feelings*. Your *feelings* change according to life's circumstances.

The job you did not get, the exam you failed, your lack of income, brings on those negative thoughts. *I will never get a job or pass that exam. I will never have enough income.* How about the good things in life?

When you got the job, passed the exam, received more income you **felt** great, uplifted, happy and positive and this is the **secret** of success when using affirmations. You need to link positive *feelings* to your goal or desire. This adds to the power of **attraction** from your mind to the universe.

Affirmations, when charged emotionally with positive *feelings*, are able to tap into your subconscious and access the unlimited power of the universe which helps create and manifest your desires and goals.

Affirmations and Visualisations

Adding your positive *feelings* to your affirmation creates a feeling of expectancy and excitement. By including the power of visualisation you can increase further the power to attract into your lives what you desire. Visualisation is a powerful tool in the armoury of manifesting. Here you can visualise or picture exactly what it is you desire in your life. You control your thought process so you can change the picture. You are the producer and the director. You hold the script.

Be specific - Imagine (imaging) exactly what it is you desire. Maybe it is good health. Then picture yourself well and healthy. See yourself well and whole. ***Feel*** better - ***feel*** fit. Repeat the affirmation - **My body *feels* great - I am well and healthy.** This positive affirmation and visualisation supports that which you desire. If you have a condition that is severe, using this positive affirmation and visualisation each day adds positive energy to your body's intelligence which will work hard to support your well-being. Maybe it is a job you are looking for. Again visualise yourself as already in the job. You have your own desk or workspace.

See yourself working away, *feeling* happy at what you are doing. Listen to the praise of your employer saying how well you are doing. Picture and *feel* yourself taking home a good income. This happened to me when I heard that a supervisory role would become vacant. I felt that I would like the job. I believed I had the experience and qualifications.

In my mind I constantly visualised myself sitting at my desk and sorting out things as they came along. I repeated to myself on a daily basis for almost a year – *its great having this new job. I am doing so well and have a good salary to go with it*. When the vacancy came up, nine people applied and you guessed it – I got the job and a good salary. (Trust me it works)

Wording Affirmations

The wording of affirmations and the level of *feeling* and visualisation that goes into it, determines the result you have.

This book is filled with positively-charged affirmations under which guidance is written to support the affirmation. Should you desire to write your own affirmation (I would encourage you to do so) then consider the affirmations below.

- I *feel* well and whole

- It *feels* great to be a non-smoker

- Income flows steadily into my life

- I love my new home

Each of these positive affirmations has one thing in common – they are all written in present time. Adding a **feeling** and visualisation to any of these is a sure way of attracting them into your life. This goes for all affirmations. (Make them short and be specific).

The **secret** of accessing that power within lies in the use of positively charged, uplifting affirmations and when linked to visual positive feelings adds support to the affirmation. For example, *I visualise myself as well and healthy and I **feel** great for it.* The use of adding feeling to your affirmations is a sure-fire way of accessing and releasing the power within you.

Using positive affirmations on a regular and daily basis strengthens your link to the power within, creating in you a belief system that is built upon the results of **you** experiencing the outcome of **your** goals or desires.

On the following pages you will find some useful and very empowering starter affirmations and positive habits which will help you to connect to your power within.

I trust that power within
and it will work with me.

The power within works
with me at all times.

*I **feel** more confident*
and self-assured.

My patience will bring
me wonderful results.

My career will be
very successful.

Income comes easily
into my life.

*I know and **feel** that*
I am getting there.

People will contact me
for my skills.

I am creating my own
positive future.

I am special and unique and
*it **feels** great to know that.*

The more I give in life
the more I receive.

I am a perfect channel
for creating new ideas.

Each day is an opportunity
to grow successfully.

Each day I will find
something good in life.

How about creating
these habits

LISTENING   CARING   LOVING   SMILING

CHEERFULNESS   GRATEFULNESS   PATIENCE

GENEROSITY   MEDITATING   EXERCISING

GRATITUDE   KINDNESS

EATING SENSIBILY

SUPPORTING OTHERS

BEING POSITIVE   TAKING TIME OUT

LOVING YOURSELF   ACCEPTANCE

BELIEVING IN YOURSELF

CREATE A KNOWING THAT YOU CAN
ATTRACT SUCCESS INTO YOUR LIFE

YOU WILL ALWAYS
GET WHAT YOU ASK FOR!!!

The important thing to remember when applying the techniques of positive affirmations is that the universe is governed by perfect, natural laws which obey the instructions given to it through the subconscious mind, and to this end it is worthwhile understanding that, like a computer, we have to be specific and clear in our instructions. How an affirmation is worded will determine whether or not we help to attract our goal or desire.

For example:

> I **want** to be successful in life!!!

> I **want** to be healthy!!!

> I **want** more income in my life!!!

> I **want** to be happier in life

The universe **IS** full of abundance which includes all your goals and desires, and does not recognise the word want.

Read this analogy to help you understand the concept that all our goals and desires already exist.

Think of the hundreds of component parts that make up a car - the different types of metal, the glass, the plastic, the rubber, the wiring, the upholstery, the paint, the polish - the list seems endless. When the first motor cars were being built the manufacturer must have wondered where all the materials were going to come from?

They began to realise that the resources already existed on our planet and people around the world were discovering and producing new materials all the time – materials that could be used in the manufacture of the motor car. Now imagine taking this new car into an unexplored region where the people there had never seen a car before.

They would be amazed and possibly frightened when they saw it, and if you had tried to explain that all the parts of the car came from mother earth they most likely would not believe you and with good reason, for as they understood things, all the materials they had and worked with would not make the car that you had, and yet you knew that all the materials were there waiting to be re-sourced. It would only be a matter of belief and trust in you by them that what you claimed was true, and if the technology was explained and introduced to them, they too, in time, would know that all the resources for manufacturing a car already existed in the world!

Therefore by stating that you want this or you want that, confuses the universe for it knows that what you **want** is there for you even though you may not believe it or cannot accept it. What happens is that the universe gives you what you are asking for which is your **want.** By saying you **want** it the universe gives to you your command which is the **want.** This leaves you in that state of wanting and not receiving and you will continue **not** to **receive** until you begin to accept that what you do desire already exists.

The **secret** to attracting your goals and desires lies in using the words that the universe recognises and accepts. Learning to be patient and not to expect it immediately also helps to support your goal and or desire. In other words, allow it to happen when it is ready and not when you think it should happen. This can help you realise your goal and or desire sooner than later. Your patience in this matter brings to your mind, peace and calm, rather than . . . *I want it and I want it* *now*. By practising patience, some of my goals and desires came very quickly, so don't be surprised if this happens to you.

Take the statements below:-

> **I want to be -** successful in life.

> **I want to be -** healthier.

> **I want more -** income in my life.

> **I want to be -** happier in life

> **I want to -** achieve my goals in life

> **I want to be -** more confident

Change the statements from the previous page to read as follows.

> **I am** successful in life

> **I am** healthier

> **I have** more income in my life

> **I am** happier in life

> **I will** achieve my goal and desires

> **I am** more confident

The affirmations now make sense to the universe and providing that your belief affirms this then the universe will work with you.

Here are some more positive statements

It will work out alright

I know it **will** happen for me

Using these positive words reinforces the power of your affirmation. Another way is to imagine that you already have your desire or goal. Live as if it is in your life now and **feel** the excitement that your life is now much better. **Imagine and see** things coming into your life. **Picture** yourself in your new chosen role in life, doing what it is you desire most and **see** yourself being rewarded in many ways with your health, relationships, career, finances and skills etc.

DON'T LET GO OF YOUR DREAMS

AND YOUR DREAMS

WON'T LET GO OF YOU

POWERMATIONS

Powermations are powerful bullet points to re-mind you how affirmations work

Present time - Your affirmation is made power-ful and effective when it is stated in the here and now. Know that they already exist. For example – *I am very successful in life! Each day brings me something positive.*

Feelings - Use positive *feelings* to reinforce your affirmation. Feel that it is already here. Feel good about it. Feel it will happen.

Visualisation - Picture yourself receiving and/or living your goal or desire. For example – *Just what I desired came my way and I see myself happy and contented.*

Repetition – Practise helps makes it happen. It is so important to understand that repetition is the gateway to fruition. Repetition imprints on your subconscious, your affirmation which it works hard to obey and carry out.

Personalise - Your affirmations must feel right. Remove any doubt from your mind. Know it will work - *feel* it will work (Trust me it does). The stronger and deeper your *feelings* are for that positive outcome the sooner you will experience the results.

Patience - Seek patience and find peace. Do not worry and do not hurry your goal or desire along. When you find peace your goals and desires will come along when the time is right.

Belief - It is necessary to have belief or faith in your affirmations for them to work for you. Your belief and faith will grow stronger as mine did.

Impress yourself - Impress your subconscious mind with your affirmation. Does it *feel* right for you? The stronger your connection with your affirmation and your subconscious, the sooner you will experience positive results.

When you experience your first result, (and you will) hang on to the *feeling*. This is the foundation on which you will build your belief and faith for all your desires.

Test your goals and desires and ask yourself these questions:

> Is it realistic?
>
> Does what I am looking for exist?
>
> Will I benefit from it?
>
> Does it *feel* right for me?
>
> Will other people benefit?

Answering *YES* to each of these, eliminates doubt and affirms that your goal and desire is worthy of becoming your reality in life.

Today's thoughts and actions are

tomorrow's attractions – make

yours positive

WHY DON'T MY AFFIRMATIONS WORK OUT FOR ME?

Over the years I have come across people who cannot understand why their goals and desires have not come about even though they repeated their affirmations on a regular daily basis! There are in my view, a number of factors which should be taken into consideration as to why a goal or desire based on affirmations does not come to fruition. When questioning some of these people, one thing became apparent.

They had read about the power of affirmations and yes they were practising them. However each person felt that because their goals and desires had not appeared when they wanted them, they were not working. A consequence of this was that their belief in them had weakened.

The energy and drive behind their belief had taken a knock because they could not see any results. Without realising it they were in a subtle way reprogramming their subconscious mind with the doubting thought of why their goals or desires were not showing up.

This thought pattern undermines the initial positive thought that, yes *my goals and desires will come my way.* This two-way thought pattern produces conflict in the subconscious mind which can only obey repeated commands, so it remains in a state of status quo. Allowing this confusion to reign as a result of lack of belief will have, depending on the feeling and/or imagination of the person, two possible outcomes. The aspiration for that desire or goal will diminish and disappear the longer you *feel* you have to wait for it and in the end nothing will have been achieved.

The second outcome and one I would encourage all to follow would be to go through the positive process of rekindling that energy for your desire or goal. This book has been written in a way which guides you through the thought process of reaching your power within from which you can generate the energy for affirming that which you desire.

In my early days of affirming I too went through phases of *When will it happen!* The great experience that I learned was to give it time – don't worry it and don't hurry it. In fact as I am writing this book one of my long term desires has come to fruition and that is the completion of my own healing sanctuary. (*This desire is over 20 years old!*) So, if you *feel* things are not happening when you want them to, hang in there and hold on to your dream.

Affirmations and other people

Affirmations are your personal goals and desires and your motive behind them can, will and does affect those around you in life. However, you need to remember that it is **your** goal and desire unless others with you have a mutually strong feeling about helping you to bring about something positive into your life.

You must be aware that a personal goal or desire to change another person's attitude or feelings toward you contradicts the Spiritual laws of life. In other words we are each special and unique individuals with free will and personal responsibility and if your goal and desire is for an individual to like you, love you or befriend you, then you are taking away that person's free will to be your friend or partner.

In a situation like this I would suggest you look at yourself. Maybe it's you who need to change your attitude and perception in life – remember, like attracts like – so visualise and see yourself attracting the right person/people into your life using the natural laws of mutual attraction. This way you honour the integrity of natural law and at the same time invoke it naturally as it should be. You are special and life has a unique way of bringing the right people into our lives at the right time.

Here are some examples of how positive affirmations have changed my life for the better - mentally, physically, financially and spiritually.

Over 45 years ago I came across an article regarding the power of positive thinking. The contents of the article centred on fate, destiny, freewill and cause and effect. It explained that to be successful in life we had to be linked in with our hidden power, have faith, and think about abundant supply, further explaining that as we think then so we are.

All this sounded strange and hard to follow but in the coming months I noticed that the things I was thinking regularly about came into my life. For example I always carried a comb around with me, and then I lost it!! What was I to do! The following day on my way to work before the shops opened I spotted a small brown paper bag lying on the footpath. I picked the bag up and inside was a brand new unused black comb (*Thank you universe*). At first I thought it was coincidence. I remembered what the article said and I set out to test the theory on small things at first and then on to bolder things.

Although I did not know then what I know now about affirmations, I was in fact building myself a belief system that was to be the foundation for manifesting and attracting into my life, health, income, success, happiness, love and healing. Listed below are just a few of the desires and goals that have come into my life as a direct result of positive affirmations.

Money to pay the gas bill. We could not afford to pay this bill and I reassured my wife that the money would come with my affirmation, *(Income will come into my life)*. Two days later when answering a knock on the door, a man by the name of Mr Wright stood there and explained that as a thank you for helping his mother and father in the past (now deceased), he would like us to accept the cheque he had in his hand. The cheque was for the exact amount of the gas bill!!

Our daughter Sallyanne needed new shoes. We could not afford any for some time. Again I said to my wife that we would find some. A few days later our friend Helen called in to see us. She had a brand new pair of child's shoes that she did not want and asked if they would fit our daughter. They were a perfect fit!

We always wanted a beautiful grey cat but when discovering the price of a kitten we knew we would not be able to afford one at that time. In my mind I held the picture of this cat and even imagined it sitting on my lap. I went down to the cat shelter to find another cat that we could give a home to. I jokingly remarked to the assistant that I would really love a grey cat. She laughed and said sorry. Another assistant passing by overheard what had been said and announced that one had just come in. We had *Bluey* for ten years! If I were reading this book for the first time as you are now, I may be thinking, all this seems a little too easy and perhaps at times a little incredible that some of the affirmations are plausible! This book has been written and based on my personal experience of practising, believing, and receiving my goals and desires.

I would like to share with you in detail and time span, my understanding of how things came into my life. Having gained an understanding as you are doing now, that life is energy and energy is life, I came to realise after studying the power of mind, that our subconscious is the key that accessed the energy of life.

How this works - and trust me it does - I can only

explain in my own way. We all know that like attracts like - for instance, when we meet someone for the first time and as the saying goes "hit it off", you *feel* that you have known each other all your life. In other words your life energies blended together - you are both on the same wavelength so to speak. We hear stories of complete strangers who make eye contact across a crowded room and for some apparent unknown reason are inexplicably drawn to each other. Coincidence! I do not believe in coincidence and it would be an interesting study as to how a couple met and matched at that particular moment, for I believe, as explained earlier in the book, that our thoughts are living energies and by sending out positive or negative thoughts will create and trigger off a series of events that will results in a conclusion either positive or negative.

Examples

Let me give you some examples of how this has worked for me. Like most homes, we have a desktop computer. As you may realise we had to agree times when we could use it. Sitting in my study, I thought how much easier it would be if I had my own computer, preferably a laptop. This is where the fun begins. I visualised, and *felt*, that I already had a laptop and that one would come my way. I did not put a time limit on this and two or three weeks had passed before a chance topic of conversation between my wife and her sister Wendy, brought a result. My wife mentioned that I was looking out for a laptop!! Wendy explained that her daughter now had a new laptop and would ask about her old one. Two days later I had my laptop. My thoughts and verbal communication had triggered off a series of events that led up to me receiving my laptop.

Another example – I work as a Spiritual Healer and Medium and take groups interested in their spiritual growth and self improvement. Early in April 2011 I took a service at a Spiritualist Pioneer Centre. During this time I was not running a group but really *felt* I would like to. Two months later I received a call from the centre asking me if I would like to take and run a Spiritual Awareness Group. This example demonstrates how our thoughts trigger off a series of events that conclude in a positive outcome. When questioning my students I enquired as to how they came to be in the group. Their answer strengthened my belief in the power of positive thoughts. More or less they each explained that they were interested in spiritual growth, but did not know where to go. Some of them said they had been asking at the centre and others heard by word of mouth. It was not a coincidence that this happened – their thoughts and verbal communication brought together through a telephone call a Spiritual Awareness Group that they were looking for and we all benefitted.

Please allow me to give one more example. One of my own and my wife Pat's goals and desires, was to own a home with some old outbuildings. Well in 2004 and not yet 55 years old, I was made redundant and retired (another desire of mine). We bought a bungalow in Lincolnshire which had lots of dilapidated outbuildings.

We had an extension built on the bungalow, by a local builder. I was going to renovate the barn and coach house myself. I knew that I had at least two years work and would require a cement mixer. This thought came to mind every time the builders came to work. This is the really great thing, for as the builder was leaving he suddenly stopped, looked at me and said "Would you like my cement mixer – I am going to buy a new one?" I still have it and it works fine. Again what has happened here is that he picked up on my thoughts for I never talked to him about my buying one and this thought process triggered off a response that was positive for me.

I do hope you found these examples I have given useful with regard to the process involved in using affirmations to support your own goals and desires and that they will encourage you to pursue and fulfil your dreams for the future.

I have stories that I could tell for all the desires and goals that came into my life as a result of using positive affirmations. Here is a list of some of them.

- Promotion at work

- Becoming a Spiritual Healer

- Tutor for Spiritual Healing

- Excellent health

- Diploma in Stress Counselling

- Owning a barn and coach house

- Retired at 55

- New home with great location

- Owned two Range Rovers

- Given a laptop computer

CHAPTER 3
SPIRITUAL LAWS OF LIFE

Spiritual laws are the natural laws of life based on virtues and values which enhance and enrich us on the many levels of mind, body and spirit. Understanding these laws can help support the affirmations for our hopes and desires. Embracing and using these natural laws can only bring positive and uplifting energy into our life.

I believe these spiritual laws always have been and always will be unalterable in that the essence of them is part of our spiritual nature which has one purpose - *"To recognise itself and to express itself as part of the energy of life"* and to help us by using these laws to create our goals and desires.

Each of us, I truly believe **IS** connected to **and** part of that energy of life. Acknowledging this allows us to utilise more fully the spiritual laws of life and the hidden potential within us, allowing us with trust, to sow the seeds of our goals and desires in the soil of the universe with a knowing/acceptance and patience, that they will bear fruit in the fullness of time.

Spiritual laws

GIVING AND RECEIVING

The motive or reason behind all that we do, say or think, determines how it will return to us through the natural law of cause and effect. *"What goes round comes round"* is one of life's true sayings. The natural law of giving and receiving works through an exchange of energy that flows through the universe. When we give unconditionally, the very act of giving this way triggers off in the energy, a response equal to or greater than the act carried out.

What goes up must come down. What goes out must come back. For example, if you had a desire to open a flower shop you would first of all have to know a great deal about flowers, what varieties, what's in season, colours, scent, how to arrange flowers etc. With this knowledge linked to your talent and desire you create a knowing and belief that you will give the best service you can, and you will treat each of your customers as special by using the spiritual laws of kindness, patience, friendliness and gratitude. In this way you are securing the success of your desire. In return, your customers will recognise your excellent customer service skills and as in all successful businesses a genuine, sincere and caring approach to a customer will bring them back to you with more custom. You can apply this to any desire and talent you have. There are many ways in which we can give and receive in life. Here are some of them.

THE LAW OF GIVING

(a) Give someone a kind word

(b) Give someone a helping hand

(c) Give a smile

(d) Give a silent blessing to all you meet

(e) When visiting, take a small gift

(f) Circulate these gifts of giving each day

THE LAW OF RECEIVING

We receive from the universe so many things and we should acknowledge them at all times.

The gift of life - the greatest gift of all

   (a) The sun and the rain

   (b) Nature and all it holds

   (c) The gift of a friend's smile

   (d) The gift of a compliment

   (e) The gift of friendship

   (f) The gift of a special skill

   (g) The gift of love

   (h) The gift of peace

Make a commitment to give and receive all that life offers and know that your inner spirit will soon grow in love and peace. Offer silently your gift of love, peace, happiness and joy each time you meet someone. Receive graciously, all that people and life offer to you, and remember the coin of a spiritual life is service. Your reward for this service helps to manifest your desires and goals.

THE LAW OF PATIENCE

(Seek patience and find peace!)

Today we seem to be living in an instant world – a world where speed seems to reign – fast food, fast delivery of orders, faster transport to get us there more quickly. Even our relationships are drawn into the ever-increasing fast pace of life.

I am sure the following will sound familiar to you.

I can't stop – I'm in a hurry

I can't stop – I have a meeting in two minutes

I can't stop – I have so much to do

The law of patience reminds us that it can bring to us great rewards, especially with regard to our goals and desires. Patience tells us to look at how we are living our life. Take time and separate those faster energies of your life into more handleable sizes.

Yes you may be working in a job or environment which places demands on you to be fast and efficient, but outside those times, learn to slow down and be patient. Be patient with yourself.

Ask yourself if it is necessary to try and pack so much into your life in one day. Will the world end if you leave something for tomorrow?

For example, does the tidying up need doing every day. Does the car need washing as soon as it gets dirty?

Patience directs your attention to nature - the apples on the trees don't rush to grow – they kind of go with the flow of life and in the end produce great results. When we recognise and embrace the law of patience, we realise that we too can go more with the flow of life.

We can take time out and be out of time so to speak. We can, through patience, learn that some things can wait until another time – your time – the time you choose and in that time you will find something very precious – something we all desire. Peace ….. perfect peace.

Embrace the energy of peace and it will show you that patience and peace can actually draw to you, your goals and desires sooner than you expected, simply because you begin to know that worrying and hurrying in life acts as an obstacle to your goals and desires. Patience and peace will change your mind energy to, *"It will happen when it's ready"*, rather than *"I want it to happen now"*.

Seek patience and find peace

Trusting in the outcome of a desire or goal is so very often sacrificed in the experiences of our past. Our fears and uncertainties of the future are there as a result of previous lack of achievement or goals. We have a desire or goal and so very often what happens after a while – weeks, or even months, our ego says to us, "Where is it, why hasn't it happened? I have waited so long! *I want it now!"* Remember this affirmation - *seek patience and find peace.*

When our memories of past experiences kick in, the fear and anxiety of it not happening for you *Now* can put a block on your goal or desire. Think of a plant. You planted it and you knew it would grow. Keep pulling the plant out to check if it is growing and you have ended the goal and intention of the plant to reach its full potential. You have to be patient and allow your goals and desires to grow.

When we create a knowing inside, we find peace and detachment. We gain trust in the outcome. You have also to be willing to allow it not to work out the way you wanted, for with the peace you find through detachment of the outcome, infinite possibilities may come to you in different ways. Things start showing up in your life that you did not expect. Opportunities come your way that will benefit you. You may look back at your original goal or desire and realise that through the patience which brought you inner peace, many more beneficial things have come into your life spiritually, physically and materially.

Patience

Be patient with yourself – what's the rush? Be patient with others – the waiter/waitress who is rushed off their feet, the queue at the bank (the cashier may be doing their best), the queuing up to be served at the checkout, the queue at the traffic lights – they won't change more quickly by you being impatient.

Be patient when showing others how to do something. They may not be as quick at learning as you are.

Be patient with the elderly – their body or mind may not be as young as yours.

Be patient with your goals and desires

Be patient with life (go with the flow of life)

Remember this affirmation - *seek patience and find peace!*

The Laws of Kindness

Kindness is a wonderful virtue. When people show kindness I believe they have recognised someone or something such as an animal, bird, fish, flower, tree etc as being in need of an uplifting energy (yours) and by being kind in this way demonstrates, even though you may not be aware of it, a subtle connection on a spiritual level. The energy of kindness expressed, supports those who need it. For example, people, animals and nature.

Kindness

Be kind to all you meet regardless of who or what they are.

Be kind to those who are grumpy or unpleasant - they may be like that for a genuine reason. Your kindness may be just the upliftment they need at that time.

Be kind to all animals of the land, birds of the air and fish in the sea.

Be kind to nature for she gives us much pleasure and beauty.

Be kind to the land. Care for it, for it nourishes us in many ways.

Be kind to the checkout person who helps pack your goods. Be kind to the person who you feel is a dropout or down-and-out. Maybe this is their pathway in life. Be kind to yourself and remember this affirmation:

Kindness returns kindness!

THE LAW OF ACCEPTANCE

This law asks us to look at what life has given us physically, mentally, materially and spiritually. Very often in life when things or circumstances do not seem right, we cast our thoughts around to look for someone or something to place the blame or reason on. For example, if we have a cold, someone gave it to us *(or maybe you received it because your immune system is low because of lack of sleep/rest/peace and quiet etc)*. You may think your body is too thin or too fat. *(Have you not been eating enough? Do you eat too much?)* Your car breaks down often. *(Is it serviced regularly?)* These are just a few simple examples of how we tend not to look to ourselves for a reason why it has happened to us.

In the greater scheme of life many lessons of life come to us in various forms, both positive and negative. We are happy and relaxed when life is going our way. If it is not we become anxious and fearful. Use the negative experiences to look at how you can benefit. There is always a lesson to learn. For instance, someone who has never been ill and becomes ill would begin to understand what illness is. They could learn the lesson of compassion. A person who was wealthy and lost their wealth would learn the lessons of poverty and humility and that sharing and caring can bring a more important type of wealth.

Positive acceptance

Remember also to accept all the good things that are in your life - your health, your relationships or material things. This book encourages you to recognise positive acceptance. You are worthy of expecting the best in life. By using the power of affirmations you honour your worthiness and commitment to expecting and receiving the best. We all earn what we attract into our lives so when something great comes your way accept it graciously and say thank you to the deliverer and the universe.

Affirmation: *I accept I am worthy to receive the highest and best that life can offer and recognise the true meaning of positive acceptance.*

Law of Detachment

Detach or to let go is an important aspect of spiritual law. It does not mean forgetting your desire or goal. Use your affirmations daily to nurture your desire and goals. Then allow the universe to work with you and for you. You have clearly stated your desire and intention. You have planted your seeds in the soil of the universe and cleared the ground by your motive and intention to use what comes your way for your benefit and the benefit of all.

Relinquish your time attachment to the outcome. Remember in my personal message from Tom (page IX - *The Wisdom of a Father*) where the father said to his son, you pull the plants out and you pull out the potential for them to grow. Therefore don't worry or fret that your goals and desires will not come to fruition. **Know** that the seeds of your desire and intention **will** grow into what you desire. Do not pull them out of the soil of the universe. Remember – detach from the time element, and let life take its course.

The law of desire

Our desire or wish for something has, for it to be realised, to be linked with the natural law of intention which basically means our aim or purpose directed by thoughts from our mind. For example, we have a strong desire to learn to swim. The desire could be strong, but, without the energy of intent, i.e. directing our thoughts for a specific aim or purpose, in this case swimming, we have a desire, but do nothing about it. By applying the law of intention we inject energy and focus into our desire and we find ourselves down at the pool carrying out our desire - learning to swim.

This law of intention applies to all our desires and goals in life and without intention or purpose our desires will remain desires. We have to realise that intention kick-starts our desire, so, whatever your desire is – to open that flower/hairdressing/DIY shop or just to develop your own potential, remember you need intention. Your motive behind your desire and intention is a driving force which will give you energy to reach your goals or aims. Ensure that your motive is for the benefit of all and you will engage the law of desire and intention.

The law of intention

Definition: To have a purpose or aim - to intend. The application of a thought directed towards creating a result. What this law of intention is saying to us is that whenever we choose to do something, the idea has to start in our mind and will remain in our mind as an idea until we choose to act upon it. When that time comes for us to carry out our idea, a subtle but noticeable change takes place within the energy of the mind.

For example, we intend to decorate a room. That's the idea. Next, our purposeful thoughts focus on what we need, i.e. the paint, wallpaper, paste brushes etc. The thoughts are still in our mind until the power of intention kick-starts that idea into action by you deciding to act upon it by physically going down to the store, purchasing your goods and physically creating a newly-decorated room.

Intention is part of the energy of life and by tapping into this energy we can direct it for the benefit of our goals and desires. Creating positive thoughts in our mind helps to bring about *(by the technique of affirming),* our goals and desires.

The law of gratitude

The law of gratitude encourages us to be grateful for everything in life. Everything from wakening up in the morning with a roof over our heads to being able to boil hot water for our first coffee of the day. There are many things in life that we may take for granted - the shoes on our feet, the clothes on our back, the car in the driveway, our family and friends.

Being grateful for all that life offers including those negative things, can bring to us a greater appreciation that there are good things in life that maybe we did not see before. Why not create a list as I have - *Positive things that came my way.* All the positive things that came my way go on my list. For example, offer of work, call from a friend, a gift, etc. After a while you will see that many good things have come into your life, and before you know it your list will grow and so will your gratitude.

CHAPTER 4
AFFIRMATIONS

The following pages are full of positive and powerful affirmations to help you create your goals and desires in life. I have listed the affirmations in specific categories with a spiritual and general category at the end. I have added throughout the pages, some powerful visualisation exercises to help you link in to your own potential. These visualisations have the added value of reinforcing your desires and goals and when reading before practising them, imagine a gentle and calm voice talking to you personally and encouraging you to believe in your affirmation. My desire is for you to realise and receive your desire and goal. Now it is your turn to start creating your desires and goals.

I wish you every success and I know you can attract those positive energies into your life, so go ahead and start affirming!

Choosing an affirmation at random

Very often in life we have more than one goal or desire - we just need some guidance to help us make a decision. If this is the case try this method that I use: close your eyes and say to yourself, *what is it that I need in my life to create balance and harmony?*

Hold one finger on the page where the affirmations start and with another finger open the book on any of the affirmation pages. Look at them and allow one of the affirmations to stand out from the rest. That is the one you need at that time.

And remember -

the future is there for those who

believe in their affirmations

CHAPTER 5
AFFIRMATIONS FOR HEALING

For me, Healing affirmations have to pave the way for other affirmations, for if we do not enjoy good health it can be hard to get motivated to think or do anything. If you are feeling well and healthy at this moment in time, that's great. Just go to any section that you wish to work on in your life but may I suggest you consider choosing a healing affirmation to start your day, as I do. Affirming that you are well and healthy helps to reinforce and strengthen your immune system which helps to keeps colds, virus and illnesses at bay.

Visualisation –
Haven of Healing and Peace

Here is a powerful and beautiful visualisation that can support your healing affirmation.

Find yourself a quiet place where you will be undisturbed for 10 to 15 minutes (longer if you wish). Although not necessary, you may find it beneficial to play some quiet, gentle music. Relax in your favourite chair or lie down and close your eyes.

Once you are relaxed, focus your mind on your breathing. Breathe in as deeply as you are able. As you breathe in, picture a ray of light entering your body. This light is the energy of the universe.

Feel its healing power relaxing your mind and your body. When you **feel** calm, breath slowly and gently. Picture in your mind a beautiful, tranquil and serene place. It could be by the sea, in the country, on a mountain, on a lake or in the desert. You choose – it's your special place. Whatever or wherever your quiet haven is, you **feel** safe, secure and at peace.

As you look around your special retreat you notice a seat or chair. This seat or chair looks so inviting that you know you want to sit down and enjoy its comfort. Once you are sat down you begin to **feel** more energised than you ever have before. You **feel** and see yourself surrounded by the most beautiful colours imaginable.

Each part of your body attracts one of the healing colours of life bringing healing and strength to that part. If you have a particular condition, focus your mind on that area. **Feel** the healing energy being directed there. Observe and **feel** that area being healed. **Feel** your whole body being ener-gised while you enjoy your experience of healing in your chosen place.

Stay there as long as you like. When you **feel** it's time to return, give thanks to the universal heal-ing energy of life and know you can return there any time you choose. Focus once more on your breathing, being aware of the world around you. Open your eyes and **feel** refreshed, well and whole.

Affirmation - *"I close my eyes and see myself as a picture of perfect health"*

Healing Affirmations

Affirmation - *"For those in need, I am a perfect channel for healing"*

We each have within us the potential to channel the healing energy of life. When you come across a person or animal that needs healing, take some time out and visualise them being surrounded by a wonderful ray of healing energy and give thanks to the Great Spirit that you have acted as the perfect healing channel.

Affirmation - *"My body is full of health and vitality"*

Visualising and picturing yourself in good health is an excellent way of supporting your immune system. **Feel** great. **Feel** well. Act well. Your body's intelligence will respond to your command and support good health.

Affirmation - *"I have a healthy diet and eat the right food. I feed my body. I feed my Spirit"*

By eating a healthy diet you nourish your mind, body and spirit. Recognise that your body is the temple of the soul and looking after it ensures it will remain well and healthy.

Affirmation - *"I love my inner child - my inner child loves me"*

The inner child is that part of us which secretly exists in our mind. It is the part of us that so often holds the reasons why we are like we are. Those past experiences which caused us so much pain, grief, hurt and sorrow are the issues that hold us back from moving on in life. Learn to love that inner child. Forgive and forget. Allow the tears to flow and with them the past hurt and grief. All your inner child wants is a love and a hug from you.

Affirmation - "*Healing energy is always available and it's there waiting for me*"

As you sit quietly, visualise the highest and best healing energy of life radiating all around you. **Feel** it, sense it and know it is always there for you. The healing energy of the universe is always available. It is there waiting for you to receive it. Just follow the advice for your affirmation.

Affirmation - "*I am a perfect healing channel*"

Those healing angels of light now channel the highest and best healing energy through me to my patient, from Spirit, through Spirit and to Spirit.

You who desire to be a healing channel can be that by employing your love, compassion and empathy. Allow your love for others to be the trigger for accessing the healing energy.

Affirmation - *"I feel the healing energy creating balance and harmony in my life"*

*My mind, body and spirit **feel** well and whole.
I FEEL my mind spirit and body glowing with health and vitality.*

Self healing is wonderful and beneficial on all levels, whatever part of you needs healing. Visualise a ray of healing energy surrounding your very being.

Affirmation - *"I send healing out into the world"*

I know in my heart and in my spirit that someone or something in the world is now benefitting from my healing thoughts.

By sending healing thoughts into the world you are acting as an Angel of Light. The world is blessed by people like you.

Affirmation - *"I make the world a better place"*

I see the world as a beautiful place - so full of life, love and healing.

You have decided to make the world a better place

and you have already. Your healing thoughts send a positive ripple of healing energy out to the world.

Affirmation - *"I radiate peace to the world"*

My loving thoughts filled with peace act as a soothing balm upon the world. (Blessed are the peacemakers for they shall bring peace)

You are the peacemaker. You have made it so by your decision to radiate peace to the world. One, who does this, helps to reduce conflict and discord and replace it with love and harmony.

Affirmation - *"I listen to my body. It knows best"*

I now listen to my body's needs. I rest more. I relax more. I look after my body and my body looks after me.

Your body knows what it needs and listening and recognising the signs is the way to creating balance in your life. Go with your feelings. How do you feel now? Awake and energised? Awake but tired? Do you feel relaxed or stressed and upset? Are you happy or sad? Are you underweight or overweight? Your body knows when it needs rest, something to eat, or less to eat.

CHAPTER 6
AFFIRMATIONS FOR SUCCESS

Everyone enjoys being successful in some area of their life. Success comes in many guises. For some it could quite simply be passing their driving test. For others it could come in the form of being the managing director of a multinational company. In between these two extremes are various levels of success for everything and anything we do in life. Affirmations based on success are a wonderful way of helping you to reach out and attract success in your life on all levels.

On the following pages you will find specific affirmations specially devised to suit a particular area in which you desire to be successful. Try the visualisation technique and enjoy it for what it is – an opportunity for you to access your power within.

Visualisation – success is already here

As with the first visualisation exercise, find that quiet place at your chosen time. Make yourself comfortable and relaxed by sitting or lying down. Play some gentle music if it helps and give yourself 10-15 minutes (longer if you wish). As before, start by focusing on your breathing. Breathe as deeply as you are able. Breathe in the wonderful energy of life and allow it to embrace your very being. Breathe out love and healing to the world.

When you begin to **feel** calm and tranquil allow your breathing to become slow and gentle. Picture yourself or imagine you are looking through an open window to the world.

You can see all the people working away and going about their business. As you scan your eyes around, you suddenly see yourself in the successful role you desire. You observe yourself in the most successful way, doing what it is you love.

You **feel** the success you observe. You become the success you desire. You are the success. You are now the director of the scene. You are the creator of your success and you **feel** on top of the world.

As the picture unfolds you become part of the scene. You find yourself working and acting successfully in your chosen desire. It **feels** real and it feels great. You **feel** energised and motivated in your success and you know that your affirmations will support your desire to be successful.

You know that you will motivate yourself and move forward in life with your goal and desires waiting for you. Keep this positive image in your mind when you return from your visualisation. Become aware of your breathing and the world around you. You **feel** refreshed and energised with the **feeling** of success in your mind. You are motivated to move forward and help create it. The following affirmations are designed for attracting success in your many areas. Look at the headings for guidance and direction.

Business, Career and Work Affirmations

Affirmation – *"The job and career I desire is on its way"*

I am working in the job of my dreams. The people are great. My salary is great and I am very thankful.

You have in your mind the job or career you would like. Hold in your mind the picture of you doing that job or career. Imagine you are happily working there and being successful. **Feel** yourself doing and enjoying the work. Your **feelings** give added support to that which you desire.

Affirmation – *"My creativity brings success"*

My creativity comes from within and from this, success will follow. My creative talents flow easily from me in many forms. I create and offer to the world, new and unique experiences which bring me success on many levels.

Affirmation - *"I am highly motivated"*

I now feel highly motivated and full of energy. I know I will achieve my goals.

Motivation is the driving force for attaining your goals and desires. It is the inner energy that fuels your passion. **Feel** energised. Act energetically and your motivation will drive you onward to your goal.

Affirmation - *"I act as a magnet to success"*

*It **feels** great the way that positive things turn up in my life. My goals and desires come easily into my life and because I share what I have, more comes my way.*

Feeling and believing that you are a magnet for success, intensifies the energy of the universe. You act and live the success you are after. It becomes part of you, especially if your success will bring benefit to those around you and the world at large.

Affirmation - *"My skills bring me success in life"*

*My skills bring to me success in life. I see and **feel** people seeking my special skills.*

We all have skills in life. Baking a cake is a skill just the same as building or engineering. Whatever your skill is, just know that it or they can bring success in your life. Believe in your skills. **Feel** that success is on its way.

Affirmation - *"New positive doors of life are opening for me"*

*I **feel** the energy and light shining for me through the opening doors of opportunity and experience. I know that I will walk positively through them to new adventures and new beginnings.*

Even as you repeat this affirmation know that you are opening the doors of your future. Your belief and feeling in affirmations opens doors that will bring to you, your heart's desire and success in life.

Affirmation - *"I believe in myself"*

I have confidence, self-assurance, love, empathy and a belief that I will succeed. My belief in myself is the foundation for my future.

Belief in oneself is a beautiful gift on its own. Conceive it, believe it, and receive it.

Affirmation - *"Today's positive thoughts create my tomorrow's positive world"*

My today's thoughts attract my tomorrow's goals. For me my goals are there. I just need to pick them up.

Thoughts are living energies and create physical form. By creating positive thoughts of what your goals and desires are and imagining or imaging them as having happened, attracts the power that brings them to you. Think positively for a brighter future.

Affirmation - *"I am the perfect person for that job"*

I see myself already in this job and I am very happy.

What you are saying here is that you recognise you have all the skills and attributes necessary to handle the job and this includes people skills. All will benefit when you are in this position.

Affirmation - *"My interview for the job will be successful"*

I shall enjoy my interview, giving my best at all times. My warm personality and knowledge will bring me success.

Interviews can be very stressful but not for you. You remain positive, calm and collected. The warmth of your smile, your self-assured confidence and knowledge, impress the interview panel.

Affirmation - *"My business grows from strength to strength"*

The way I handle my business and treat people, ensures the success of my business.

See yourself as a great business person. You recognise the importance of being kind and caring to your staff, customers and clients. This is what helps bring success to businesses. As you give your best service, people respond by giving you their service.

Affirmation - *"My employer recognises and rewards my hard work and skills"*

*I see myself being rewarded for all my positive efforts. It **feels** great. I am more motivated than ever.*

The effort you put into your work combined with a positive, cheerful disposition, draws the attention of those in charge. They recognise your hard work and linked with your positive approach and attitude, know that your value to them should be rewarded.

Affirmation - *"My new business will be a great success"*

My new business is going great and I am attracting the right people to make it a success. I give thanks to the universe for all of this.

No matter what your new business is, see and **feel** it taking off. **Feel** the support given to you by all concerned. **Feel** and express your excitement for this new challenge and direction in life knowing that it will be successful.

Affirmation - *"My career brings me success and happiness"*

My career opens up the door of opportunity. My hard work and commitment will bring me much success.

Your chosen career and your strong desire to do well is a perfect platform for your future growth. See yourself working enthusiastically and enjoying what you do. See yourself moving up the ladder of success, reaching and attaining your goals and desires.

CHAPTER 7
AFFIRMATIONS FOR RELATIONSHIPS

Visualisation: Tree of life

Using the techniques suggested in the previous visualisations, picture yourself surrounded by all the people who you love in your life. Imagine that you are the centre of the tree of life and as you open your arms wide like the branches of the tree, see yourself embracing your family and friends. **Feel** love and friendship with them all.

Feel that your relationships are well-balanced with give and take from both sides. Communication is important to you in relationships, so visualise yourself enjoying quality time with all your family. You give love and understanding to all of your loved ones who respond in turn by giving to you, love and respect. You know that all those in your life, like you, are unique individuals and to this end you visualise each person as special and precious and part of the wonderful tree of life. Your love draws them to you and as you embrace them, see them embracing you as you and they become as one with the tree of life.

Affirmation - *"I have a wonderful partner"*

*My partner loves and cares for me. This makes me **feel** special and I love him/her more for this.*

By choosing this affirmation you have recognised the love and energy of someone close to you. Remind yourself always of this and you increase the bond of love between you. When you love someone in this wonderful way it is because you see yourself in them. Their acts of kindness and love are a reflection of you.

Affirmation - *"I allow my partner to be them-selves"*

We each grow in our own space. Knowing that the roots of love bind us together allows us to be free and yet share the same pathway.

Allowing your partner to be themselves is a sign that you are happy and comfortable and able to trust your partner. Because you know they love you, you have found one of the great secrets of partnerships.

Affirmation - "*I express myself in a loving and caring way*"

*I now express my **feelings** and thoughts in a caring, thoughtful way and my partner sees me as loving and kind.*

You were meant to express yourself in a loving and caring way, for this is the way of the spiritual warrior and by acting in this way you will attract love and caring into your life.

Affirmation - "*I forgive and set myself free*"

My forgiveness has lightened the emotional burden I carried and now I feel light-hearted and free from stress, pain, grief and sorrow.

Forgiveness of self and others is a great healer. You have recognised that you can forgive and the time has now come for you to move on to higher things. Your Relationship can only benefit.

Affirmation - *"I am willing to change"*

I now have more patience and tolerance, kindness and generosity. My willingness to change will make me a better person.

Your willingness to change is a sign that you have recognised a change in your thought pattern. You have glimpsed something greater in yourself. Something or someone has touched your soul and you feel that something new, something brighter within, is coming your way. From this change your relationship grows stronger.

Affirmation - *"I think before I speak"*

My thoughts are always clear, and I know what it is I wish to say. I think before I speak.

You have learned the valuable lesson of examining your thoughts before speaking. Thinking first gives you the opportunity of deciding what you really want to say and now you choose to retain your energy and clarity of thought before speaking.

Affirmation - "*I am very forgiving*"

I forgive myself, and I forgive others. This brings to me, peace of mind and comfort of the body.

Forgiveness brings so much relief and peace of mind. Acknowledging that you are forgiving means that you are prepared to let go and move on for yourself and others. Forgiving ourselves and others for past issues releases blocked, negative, emotional energies. Forgiveness brings to you a genuine healing energy that repairs the past and prepares a new future.

Affirmation - "*My relationships grow stronger and more loving each day*"

My relationship with people is stronger than ever. We bond and blend together, creating unity for all.

We all have relationships at home, work, and socially. Relationships are challenging and give endless opportunities for personal and spiritual growth. The secret to all relationships is to allow with love, others to be who they desire to be and for you to be who you desire to be.

Affirmation –"I listen to others but think for myself"

*I allow my **feelings** to guide me. I listen to what others say but I make the choice that I **feel** is right for me.*

How many times in life have people told you what is best for you and what you should do? This affirmation is saying *listen to what others tell you, but decide and do what you desire to do*. You are the only one who knows how you **feel** about anything. Allow your **feeling** to direct you. Seek advice yes, but make the final decision yourself.

Affirmation - "*There is someone in the world waiting just for me*"

I see myself in a happy relationship with some-one kind, loving, caring and generous and it feels great.

We each have someone in the world waiting for us. By searching too hard saying "*I can't find my right partner*", works against what your desire is. Focus in your mind as already having that caring, loving and sharing person in your life. **Feel** and imagine the energy of someone close to you.

Picture yourself enjoying life with just the right person for you. Know that the mutual law of attraction brings together like-minded people.

Affirmation - "*I now communicate more with my partner*"

I talk more with my partner and we both feel happier.

Communication in all partnerships is one of the most important elements for a successful relationship. By choosing to talk to your partner and expressing your **feeling** about any issue, allows your partner to understand you more and why you **feel** and act as you do. This bridge-building is the saviour of relationships for as relationships cement their love and understanding of each other they grow closer and closer, happier and happier.

Affirmation - "*I am no longer possessive of my partner*"

I now release my partner from my possessiveness and know this will bring us closer. This is my heart's desire.

What you are saying here is that you now recognise your partner as being a person and not an object to possess. You realise that they have their own unique traits and personality and cannot be owned. You know they love you and you can therefore let them be free to be who they want to be and not what you want them to be, i.e. caged with their wings clipped.

Affirmation - *"I am no longer jealous of my partner"*

Now I see my partner as my equal – someone I enjoy sharing life with, without fear or mistrust.

Unfounded fear and mistrust can destroy relationships. Allow the reassurance from your partner to eliminate that fear and trust. Learn to build trust and your relationship will flourish. Jealousy causes so much heartache in relationships that it can destroy them. Letting go of jealousy allows you and your partner to be two individuals each experiencing life their own way and yet having unconditional support from each other.

Affirmation – *"I love my partner"*

Acknowledging that you love your partner is the

truest expression of love and comes from the spirit within. This brings into your life, harmony peace and happiness.

Affirmation - *"My partner is also my best friend"*

My partner is not just the person I love; they are also my best friend

We all have someone with whom we are meant to be with as a partner - someone we can love and someone who will love us. To have them as a best friend adds another dimension to your relationship. Best friends share things that they often don't, with their partner. This can lead to a more open and fulfilling relationship.

This is one of my favourite affirmations. I print these out on business cards and give them out to people when it feels right to do so.

Something positive is about

to happen in my life

and I feel good about it

CHAPTER 8
AFFIRMATIONS FOR WEALTH

Visualisation

Sometimes in life we can feel that scarcity in our finances is to be our lot in life! Understanding affirmations can help to induce a more positive outlook that states *"abundance in life comes to me in many ways"*.

Using this positive visualisation supports your desire to see and experience greater abundance in this area. Again carrying out the visualisation techniques, imagine, see and feel yourself as already receiving abundance in life - materially and financially.

See yourself and your skills being called for and rewarded with much abundance. See yourself sharing your wealth freely and unconditionally and observe that as you share your wealth this way so you open the doorway for more wealth to come to you. Create in your visualisation, a feel good factor for all the good that you have done with your wealth. As you see yourself giving freely so you see that the universe returns your generosity tenfold.

Affirmation - "*I always have money to give away*"

My generosity always ensures that I will always be repaid positively in many different ways.

Life has a wonderful way of repaying us for the kindness we show when we are unconditionally generous. When we give in this way we find that the generosity of the universe repays us back in many ways. *"And all your needs will be met".*

Affirmation - "*I am a very generous person*"

My generosity returns to me tenfold. I share with the world and the world shares with me.

Generosity is life's way of saying, "I like to give and I like to share". Your generosity is a special gift. You give and share easily and for this, life will share with you. This is the spiritual law of giving and receiving. You will never go without when you are generous in the world.

Affirmation - *"I always have money in my purse or wallet"*

I believe in the abundance of life and I will never go short.

Believing and repeating this affirmation sends out a signal to the universe that will respond accordingly. Abundance and not scarcity is the thought in your mind. Know and **feel** that the universe will take care of you. Trust in the outcome.

Affirmation - *"It's alright for me to have the good things in life"*

I enjoy what I have and I deserve to have them and when I share what I have, more comes my way.

Life is meant to be full of abundance from which we share. There is no need to feel guilty about having these good things. When you have the abundance of life you are in a position to share and the more you share the more you receive. So go on giving and receiving.

Affirmation - *"I conceive it. I believe it. I receive it"*

I do believe and I know I will receive. I have no doubt. I trust and it will work out.

Thoughts are things. They are ideas we have behind our goals and desires. <u>Conceiving</u> them is the first step. Create in your mind what it is you are looking for. Be specific. Spell it out in your mind. Be bold. Be positive. <u>Believe.</u> Do not doubt that you can achieve your goals and desires. Live them in your mind. **Feel** it as if it is already there. <u>Receive</u> it. Be prepared to receive it in your life when the time is right.

Affirmation - *"I have all that I need (and more)"*

*Each day I look around, I see abundance in my life. I am short of nothing and it **feels** great.*

Accepting that you have all that you need is the most wonderful signal you can give to the universe. You have acknowledged the abundance of life. You know you will never go short.

Affirmation - "*I always have income from somewhere*"

My skills will always ensure that income will come into my life and no matter what, I will have what I need.

Financial security in life is a concern to millions of people around the world, but not for you. As you place trust in this affirmation you will discover that you will be provided for from the many sources of life.

Affirmation - "*I prosper wherever I am*"

Wherever I am in life I prosper. I attract to me the abundance of life which provides all my needs.

Believing in this affirmation allows you with confidence, to go anywhere. You know you will prosper for you have made it so, by your power of positive thinking.

Affirmation - "*Even now greater things await me in the universe*"

The universe provides all that I need at all times.

This affirmation confirms your belief that the universe will provide. This powerful statement is your way of saying *thank you*. The universe replies - *You are welcome!* Your inner knowing has grown to such a degree that you have created a field of positive energy all around. You are that magnet for success.

I believed and

I received

CHAPTER 9
POSITIVE CHARACTER
AFFIRMATIONS

Visualisation

Feeling good about ourselves gives us confidence and courage to handle the many issues that life throws at us, but how many of us have that confidence and self assurance?

By following and introducing this visualisation into your life you too can experience and feel the power of positive thinking. As with the previous visualisations, place yourself in a safe, comfortable environment where you can relax easily and create in your mind the following scenario.

Imagine that you are in a cinema watching the

premier of the latest film. After the credits have rolled the opening scene shows a person who is good-looking, confident and self-assured.

You cannot see the face of the person because they have their back to you as they address a large audience. The way they talk and the stance they hold endears the audience to them. They talk in a relaxed way with great articulation.

When the person has finished, the audience give the person a warm round of applause. When they turn away from the camera you see their face and you gasp with amazement for it is you who was addressing the crowd.

You continue to watch the unfolding scenes and as you watch you realise that you are special and you can be confident. You have the ability to be like that. You begin to feel good about yourself. Your self esteem grows.

Your dignity grows and you know that you can become the person in your mind - strong, confident, assured, tactful, diplomatic, kind, generous and understanding.

You begin to see and feel a new you emerging like

a beautiful butterfly from its cocoon, and so you should, for you are special, unique and precious.

Affirmation - *"I live in a world of wonders and I am one of them"*

I acknowledge the wonder of the world and know that my love and energy help to make the world a wonderful place.

I look around the world and see beyond the rubble and chaos. I look at the beauty of the world – the new growth in the spring, the beautiful tapestry of colour in the autumn and the raindrops nourishing all life. The world is full of wonder and none more so than me. There is only one of me in the world and this is what makes me so special and wonderful.

Affirmation - *"I am a very thoughtful person"*

Kind words and warm smiles are my way of creating happiness in the world.

Being thoughtful simply means your thoughts are full. So fill your thoughts with peace and calm. Be thoughtful in a positive, caring way.

Affirmation - "*I have great belief in myself*"

I know life will work out well for me. It's already happening.

Exclaim to the universe that yes life will work out just the way I would like it. **Feel** the positive energy of the outcome. See whatever it is you are after as already being in your life.

Affirmation - "*I have the time to give to people*"

I am well-blessed for in today's busy world I make time for others. I am there to give support when needed.

The world needs special people like you – someone who has decided to share their time with others. When you have time for others then others will have time for you - a time to be listened to, a time to have a shoulder to cry on and a time to laugh.

Affirmation - "*I am a kind person*"

As I share my kindness I make people and the world feel happier.

Kindness is a virtue and in today's world this virtue is very much in demand for life is busy and noisy. By choosing this affirmation you have recognised a trait in you that is like a precious stone.

Affirmation - *"I am beautiful (I must be) - God does not make junk"*

*I now see myself as special and unique - a wonderful part of creation- and it **feels** great.*

You are beautiful for God does not make junk. It is our ego and the world that defines what is beautiful and what is not. Your eyes are the window of your soul. Let them reflect your beauty. Care not for the good intentions of others. Care only that you are a beautiful child of God and feel good about this.

Affirmation - *"I am achieving my goals"*

I see my goals and desires unfold in my mind. It won't be long before I see them in life.

We all have goals and desires and whatever yours is, **feel** as if it has happened already - the excitement - the happiness. Live these goals and desires in your mind and you will live them in life.

Affirmation - *"I am a loving person"*

My unconditional love is given freely to all I meet in life. They are blessed and I am blessed.

All you need is love. You have recognised this by choosing this powerful affirmation. You are a loving person and wherever you go your love goes. You give it unconditionally and for this you will always receive love in return.

Affirmation - *"I am a cheerful person"*

My cheerfulness keeps me happy and able to cope with life.

Your warm friendly smile and your kind words carry a powerful uplifting energy to all who you meet.

Affirmation - *"I live to love and I love to live"*

I love life and all its energy. It makes my heart sing. I love to live and I live to love.

Living to love is a sure way of bringing peace and happiness in your life. Your desire to live this way is a positive indication that you are becoming aware of your connection to the Great Spirit. Loving to live gives you the opportunity to share your love and to enjoy the rich experiences of life.

Affirmation - *"I do not worry but I do care"*

I replace worry with care. This gives me more positive energy to give help and support when needed.

By choosing not to worry, you have recognised that there are some things in life you simply cannot change, e.g. world disasters, man's inhumanity to man. Worry makes us ill, fearful and gives us a **feeling** of hopelessness. Replacing worrying with caring brings out your compassion and empathy - strong spiritual energies - which allow you to do what and when you can, with love and healing and a **feeling** of doing your best.

I do my very best

and leave the rest

Affirmation - *"The past is gone"*

I feel the energy of my new life bringing happiness

and peace to me as I now let the past go and bring a new positive future in.

The past is over and gone. I can let go. I am now creating a wonderful and bright future for myself - a future with love, laughter and healing.

Affirmation - *"I don't explain. I don't complain"*

I work quietly on the path of life, preserving my energy for the good things in life – love, peace and harmony.

Going about your business in your own quiet way and keeping your own counsel is very empowering. It puts you in charge of your life and you do not **feel** a need to complain for you accept life's experiences as soul growth. By not complaining, and explaining, you have more energy for yourself and the world.

Affirmation - *"I am precious and special"*

It's great to know that I am special. It makes me feel happy and wanted.

You are precious and you are special. Your character has and is being forged by the experience of life. Just know that you are special. It does not matter what others think of you. If God had a picture on the wall it would be one of you, for you are a precious child of God.

Affirmation - "*My confidence grows each day*"

Each day my confidence brings self-assurance and self-esteem. People see a positive change in me and I feel good about this.

You are not the person you were. You now feel more confident and more assured in all that you say and do. Your growing confidence gives you more personal power. You can say *yes*. You can say *no*. You **feel** much happier and more alive than ever before.

Affirmation - "*Each day I make a positive difference to the world*"

*I think positively and act positively. The difference is **felt** in the world by my thoughts, words and actions. The world is blessed and I am blessed.*

By choosing this affirmation you make a wonderful statement to the world.

Affirmation - *"I do not judge. I only observe"*

By choosing not to judge I become an observer in life. I see all sides but don't take sides. This brings wisdom and a greater understanding of life to me.

You have taken away a perception of what is right and wrong for you know that judgment is based upon your own values and morals. Unless we have walked in the shoes of others we cannot judge. You are now an observer, watching and viewing but not criticising, analysing or taking sides. The result of this brings to you, peace and tranquillity.

Affirmation - *"I am in control of my life"*

I respect the good intentions of others but I will have the final say. It is my choice. I live by my own decisions whether right or wrong.

You have chosen to be in control of your life. Well done. With this control <u>YOU</u> decide to say *yes I will* or *no I won't.*

Affirmation - "*I have a wonderful attitude of gratitude*"

I am eternally grateful and thankful for all I have. I don't take it for granted. I am always appreciative.

When we create, we build or form. This affirmation is asking you to be grateful for everything in your life – the shoes on your feet, the food in the cupboard, your job, car, relationship, friends, good health etc. The power of gratitude is another way of saying *"Thank you Great Spirit for all I have in life"*. The Great Spirit replies, *"You are welcome".*

Affirmation - "*I love myself first*"

I love myself first then I love everyone else, for when I have love I can give love, to everyone.

Loving yourself first is a great way of knowing that you are part of the great scheme of life. When you love yourself you love the Great Spirit called God. You are from the Great Spirit. You deserve that love. Accept it freely. **Feel** good about it.

Affirmation - "*I smile and it feels good*"

I know my smile is special. It's my gift to the world and I give it freely

When you smile you give out a radiant energy of love and those receiving your smile **feel** good inside. Your smile has a wonderful effect and it uplifts those who you smile at. Your smile can make someone's day. Your smile reflects a soul that is happy and at peace. Your smile is a precious gift to the world**.**

Affirmation - "*I become more patient every day*"

I am at peace in mind, spirit and body. There is no need to worry and no need to hurry. I just go with the flow.

Patience is a virtue and brings to you its own special gift – <u>PEACE</u>. When you are patient your mind is calm and tranquil. You have a knowing that patience ensures you are not rushing around saying *I want it and I want it now*. You know we live in an instant world but have chosen patience.

Affirmation - "I am flexible in life and go with the flow"

My flexibility brings to me many opportunities. I am recognised as someone who goes with the flow, someone whose patience and tolerance gets the job done.

Being flexible means bending without breaking. Creating patience and tolerance allows you to go with the flow of life, not worrying and not hurrying. Know you will get there with a relaxed mind, body and spirit.

Affirmation - "I find solutions to life's problems"

My character is forged by the experiences of life and I believe there is a spiritual solution to all problems.

There is a solution to all problems and recognising that problems are life's opportunities, allows us to explore and discover part of us we have never reached before.

Affirmation - *"Experience is my opportunity in life to grow"*

I love the experiences of life for they give me endless opportunities to grow and develop.

Use life's experiences to grow successfully and positively in all areas. Opportunities come in many ways – some even in a negative way. What message do they carry? A message of growth from which you can learn, i.e. job experience, caring, sharing, coping, loving, confidence-building, patience, tolerance etc. Grab those opportunities as they come. It could be just what you were waiting for to help you grow in a certain direction

Affirmation - *"I trust in the outcome"*

I trust in life and it will bring freedom to me allowing me to express myself lovingly and confidently knowing that all will turn out well.

T.R.U.S.T. - **T**o **R**eally **U**nderstand **S**pirit, **T**rust.

Affirmation - *"I speak more confidently each day"*

I do have something to say. I do have an opinion.

*I can speak out loud with the strength of my own convictions. I **feel** my confidence growing. I see myself as confident and self-assured and I will be heard.*

Self-expression is our way of talking to the world but often we find our lack of confidence suppresses our desire to talk confidently and be independent of the good intention of others. Be yourself. It is your right to express yourself.

Affirmation - "My social skills are well-developed"

My social skills endear people to me. I interact with confidence and assurance.

Social skills are the tools we need to interact confidently with others. Your self-confidence and belief in yourself allows you to socialise at all levels of business and pleasure. You talk with people not at them.

Affirmation - "It's OK if I fail"

You have not really failed. It is just not the result you wanted. See yourself as being successful in the end.

In our society today we have a culture where suc-cess and achievement is the order of the day. If we do not achieve, it is looked upon as failure. Substitute the word *failure* as simply *not having the result you would have liked* and that's OK. Maybe it is not your time yet.

Maybe there is a message for you. Do I need this anyway? The greatest thing to remember is that your inner spirit will never fail.

Believe in yourself -

you are better and more

special than

you think you are!

Affirmation - *"I remember my dreams very clearly"*

Ideas and answers come to me in my dream state and I recall them clearly.

When you need an answer to something or are looking for an idea, place your request to dream power. Just before going to sleep, spell out the problem you have or the idea you are looking for. Be specific. Hold a feeling that the answer will come. It may not be the following day but it will come if you place your trust where it works – in your mind. Keep by your bedside a note book and pen. Record the things you remember. Many people have received answers and inspiration from the power of their dreams.

Dreams are the inner visions

for our goals and desires

CHAPTER 10
SPIRITUAL AFFIRMATIONS

Visualisation

I could not leave Spirituality out of this book for I believe that we are all part of the wonderful energy of life we call God, the Great Spirit or whatever name you choose to give this essence of life. There are times in life when our material world cannot give us the answer or comfort we need.

By connecting to what I call the energy of life, we can find peace of mind and comfort of the body. In that connection we can receive the solutions to all our worries and concerns. So, join with me now for a visualisation I call *Journey to the Temple*. As you are reading go with the flow of the words and allow them to bring to you, inner calm and peace.

Imagine you can hear a voice - gentle and reassuring - encouraging you to create a most beautiful scene in your mind. Give yourself some time and space to enjoy this. When you are nice and relaxed in your favourite chair or couch, close your eyes and focus on your breathing. Breathe in as deeply as you are able. During your inhalation imagine that you are breathing in the essence of peace and love which gives you a **feeling** of calm and tranquillity. As you breathe out imagine that you are exhaling peace and love around the world. After a short time return to your natural rhythm of breathing pattern. By now you will **feel** calm and very relaxed.

Picture in your mind a pathway of your choosing. See yourself walking down this path **feeling** safe and secure. Hold on to a **feeling** that you are going to meet someone very special. You can **feel** the ground beneath your feet and the warmth of the sun on your face.

You just know it's a good place to be. You look around and observe what is there (*what do you see?*). As you continue on the pathway you see a bench or seat and **feel** drawn towards it. As you sit down a **feeling** of expectancy and excitement come across you and you begin to **feel** the loving, all-embracing energy of life surround you.

It's such a **feeling** of love that you have not experienced before and you know that you are in the presence of a great and wonderful power that brings to you, an awareness that you and all life are part of this power and love.

You **feel** as if you have come home and you now recognise that in life there is a force or energy that only wants the best for you. At this stage of relaxation send out from your thoughts any questions you may have. For instance you could say, *what changes do I need to make to improve my life*. Let your question go into the universe.

The answer may come in many ways; you may feel a desire to be more patient or to quickly resolve an issue that you can't face. Or the answer may come through someone else who may come into your life at the right time. Do not be concerned if the answer does not come when you WANT IT! Trust me it will come at the right time in the right place.

Stay as long as you **feel** is necessary, enjoying the energy of the force and love of life.

Affirmation - *"Thank you God. Thank you Great Spirit"*

I thank God the Great Spirit for simply being there for me for we are one and the same.

Recognising that you are part of God the Great Spirit gives to you a wonderful feeling of being connected to the source of all creation.

Affirmation - *"I have a choice so I choose peace and love"*

*I allow an inner **feeling** of peace and love to bring about the right choice for me in any conflicting decision.*

Life is full of choices and often we are not sure which the right choice is. When we are faced with a decision and are not sure which choice to make, consciously decide to choose peace and love. **Feel** at peace and **feel** the energy of love.

Affirmation - *"I serve the Great Spirit in all I think, do and say"*

I serve the Great Spirit in many ways - with my

thoughts, words and actions. As I serve then I too am served.

Being of service in life is the true pathway of spiritual growth. When you are in service to the Great Spirit of life, you are well blessed. Many opportunities come our way to be of service. It could be service with a smile. It could be service by helping out and supporting someone emotionally or financially.

Affirmation - *"My Angel guides draw nearer when I need them"*

As I think of my guardian angels in times of need, I know they will be there with me and for me.

The Angel guides and helpers are very often our loved ones who have passed on and when in need of support and strength, hear your call and with love and healing, give to you the energy you need to cope and resolve the issue at hand.

Affirmation - *"I know I am a child of God the Great Spirit"*

I know I am part of the great experience of life

and no matter what happens the Great Spirit will be there for me.

Knowing that you are a child of God, the Great Spirit assures you that you are never alone ever!

Affirmation - *"God the Great Spirit walks with me each step of the way"*

God walks with you and God talks with you. Know this. Each step you take, each look you take, know that the energy and life of the Great Spirit is there.

When our Spiritual awareness grows we know that the essence of the Great Spirit is in everyone and everything. We see and recognise this in all that is around us. This brings to us love, peace and harmony.

Affirmation - *"My belief in God the great Spirit gives me strength and healing"*

God is within me and I am within God. Together we are one.

Having a belief system based on your God has un-limited power, for you draw energy and healing from the creator of all life itself. You know you are part of God and therefore receive that strength and healing.

Affirmation - *"When I look at life I am looking at the Great Spirit"*

*My heart sings for joy when I see and **feel** the wonder of all life.*

No matter where you look, no matter who or what you look at, you are looking at the magnificence of the Great Spirit: the beautiful sunset, the wave-lapped shore, the falling leaves in autumn, the young child, the old person – you cannot be where the Great Spirit is not.

Affirmation - *"I serve the Great Spirit God in all I think, say and do"*

As I serve the Great Spirit then I too am served with love, light and healing and I am well blessed.

The Great Spirit we call God embraces all mankind and has no allegiance to any one sect or religion. Exclaiming that you serve the Great Spirit in all you think, say and do, is the most sacred thing you can do, for in serving the Great Spirit you serve life in all its diversity. You are a messenger, a teacher, a disciple, a Good Samaritan and a beautiful soul.

Repetition is the

gateway to fruition

CHAPTER 11
MORE USEFUL AFFIRMATIONS
TO HELP YOU ON YOUR WAY

*I would like to teach
the world to heal*

*My body knows best
when to rest*

*Dark skies do not
mean dark days*

*W. O.W.
World of wonders*

*Just say
thank you*

*Seek inside,
not outside*

Life is good to me

*The universe is
unfolding perfectly for me*

*Reach in, not out – that's
where the answer is*

*It's alright to receive
as well as give*

*I have a choice.
I choose peace*

*It's alright for me to have
the good things in life*

*I am unique
and special*

TRACKING YOUR
GOALS AND DESIRES

To help you keep track of your goals and desires, I have included a "goals" and "desires" chart.

This is something I have been doing for years. The idea is to sit quietly and listen to your mind and heart. What are your goals and desires? What changes would you like to come about in your life? Pencil them in with the date and when they arrive in your life, enter that date also as this will be your record for the future. You will then be able to look back and see where you were and how far you have travelled.

Write all your goals and desires down no matter how small or large. One of my earliest memories was a time during which I was experimenting. I had lost my comb and as I had a "Beatle" haircut!! a comb was essential to me to keep it looking good!!! As I was walking to work the following morning, I noticed a small, unopened brown bag lying on the footpath. Intrigued and nosy I picked it up and found a brand new black comb inside!! So - go ahead - write it all down and see what happens.

Goals and Desires chart

Goals and Desires chart
